THE
Archive Photographs
SERIES

PERSHORE

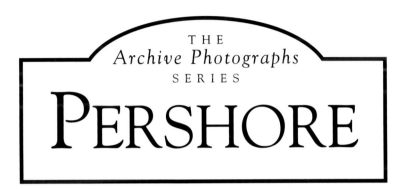

THE
Archive Photographs
SERIES

PERSHORE

Compiled by
Marion Freeman

CHALFORD

The Chalford Publishing Company
St Mary's Mill, Chalford,
Stroud, Gloucestershire, GL6 8NX

ISBN 0 7524 0726 0

Typesetting and origination by
The Chalford Publishing Company
Printed in Great Britain by
Bailey Print, Dursley, Gloucestershire

Also published in The *Archive Photographs* series:
Around Droitwich (Bob Field)
Redditch (Phillip Coventry)
Stratford-upon-Avon and Beyond (John Oldfield)
Tenbury Wells and the Teme Valley (Howard Miller)

PROPOSED TOWN HALL FOR PERSHORE. (See "Crowquill's" Jottings).

As long ago as 1909 there were suggestions for a Market Hall and Assembly Rooms to be erected in Broad Street. An estimate of £3,000 was given for a building approximating the above.

Contents

Acknowledgements

I would like to thank everyone who has given me information and loaned photographs for inclusion in this book. I have spent many happy hours collating it all and listening to stories of the old days.

My special thanks go to Ralph Fuller for his unstinting encouragement and assistance; John Annis, Peggy Maple, Ruth Partridge and George Cox and also to the following for the loan of material: Marshall Wilson and the Civic Society, Mrs Classen, Jackie Edmunds, the Heritage Centre, Mrs Win Summerton, Pershore WI, Heinz Wichmann, Doreen Peart, Bob Ashworth, Roslyn's Stores, Pinvin, Kath Townend, Jan Browning and Laurie Clifton-Crick. I would also like to thank the following for additional information: Julie Lockwood, Keith Goddard, John Hemming, Jean Glazebrook, Esme Westcott, Mr and Mrs Bundy, Liz Foxton Research, Mr Crooke and Worcester Record Office. Mr Couchman has kindly given me permission to use several of his photographs – others are by S.P. Hamill, Warwickshire, Worcestershire & Birmingham Illustrated, D. & E. Jones, Dowty & Sons, Stephen Widdowson, J. Glover, Berrows Newspapers, Evesham Journal, Fearnside and Martin.

Bibliography

The Book of Pershore, Barrett and Wilson
Yesterday's Town: Pershore, Christine Trollope
Vale of Evesham Historical Research Papers, 1977
Pershore 'Where D'ye think', Revd R.H. Lloyd
Pershore: A Short History
The Rambler in Worcestershire, John Noakes

Introduction

This book is a nostalgic look at old Pershore and the surrounding villages, while research for the text has been undertaken from many sources, as can be seen from the Acknowledgements. I am extremely grateful to all those who have helped and I do hope that I have not forgotten any of the many folk who have assisted me.

In the main, however, the information is comprised of memories from a host of individuals all of whom have patiently and helpfully enlarged my knowledge of the area. Having fallen in love with the town when we moved here over 25 years ago, I was pleased to be told recently that I was now 'almost a native'. I would add that I have never felt an outsider, not even during the first few weeks of my living here. Pershore is certainly a super place.

In fact, so much information came to hand during my research that it must be an ongoing project. As Secretary of Pershore Heritage and History Society, I am anxious that none of the information should be lost. Although I have tried not to include any stories that have not been confirmed by at least three people, it is a fact that people remember incidents differently. If, therefore, you disagree or can add to any comment in this book, do please contact me. It goes without saying that I will welcome any additional information or comments that I may be given – even if you should disagree with something I've written!

The majority of the pictures in this book have not previously been published. Those that have are included because I feel they deserved a second showing. A large selection of those which have been included are from the collection of the Civic Society and from Pershore Heritage Centre which is attempting to built up its local records.

One or two of the pictures were taken relatively recently but it is surprising how quickly one becomes accustomed to changes. While parts of the town remain relatively unaltered, others have changed beyond recognition. I hope you gain as much enjoyment from this trip down memory lane as I have had in compiling it.

Looking down High Street from approximately the position of today's Abbey Garage, c. 1900. The New Inn can be seen on the left.

Bedford House, Bridge Street, built in the early 1800s for the Bedford family. Pershore is justly proud of its many houses from this period but while it takes pride in the past, and works ceaselessly to preserve what is best, it also enjoys a lively and active present and looks forward with optimism and foresight to the future.

One
Around Pershore

The *Pisgah*, a 70ft long, 13½ft wide barge, passing under Pensham Ashes, and through the empty Weir Meadow water-gate. The lowered cabin which enabled it to pass under the low bridges of Eckington and Pershore is clearly visible. Built in Holland, it transferred in 1927 to East Anglia, trading for two years as *Nancy II*, carrying general cargo from King's Lynn. The craft was then bought by George Partridge, owner of Pershore Mill, who renamed her after the mountain from which Moses saw the Promised Land. From 1929 to 1950 the *Pisgah* was skippered by Bill Butt. He was followed by his brother Arthur, and later, by John Caddy. In July 1956 she took pride of place at the re-opening of the lock following renovations. The last vessel to ply the Avon on a commercial basis, the *Pisgah* was sold in 1974 to Mr James Ryle who took her to Bristol where she was converted to carry passengers and taken via Lands End to France for use as a holiday charter boat.

The steam launch *Bee*, towing a barge, arrives at Pershore. The *Bee* later joined by the *Wasp*, preceded the *Pisgah* and was the first steam barge on the Avon, capable of towing up to three barges. It operated between 1862 and 1917.

At a sale of possessions of the late Mr J. Glover, photographer of Bridge Street, Mr Ralph Fuller purchased some printing frames. In 1952 he discovered that one still contained a negative which he printed with the result above. Mr Fuller believes the picture was taken near the Angel Hotel landing stage some eighty years ago. There were rumours of German sailors on the Avon about the time of the First World War but nothing is known for certain about the craft or the men crewing her.

Many variations of this view have been photographed from Avon Bank showing the entrance to Pershore. This one was seemingly taken during the Second World War when two pill-boxes guarded the bridge. On the opposite bank, a field gun was set up where the horticultural pumping station now stands. Manned by the Home Guard, it had a brick-built emplacement with a gun pointing up Wick Hill. Rev J.D. Smyth, Vicar of Pinvin and curate at Pershore Abbey, had charge of the firing pin.

A plaque attached to the new bridge opened in 1926 records that the contractor was Hobraugh & Co. Ltd, with work inaugurated by Worcester County Council under the chairmanship of Lt. Col. C.F. Milward, then Chairman of the Highways and Bridges Committee. The bridge builders apparently regarded the Pershore stretch of the Avon as little more than a stream and were shocked when it flooded and much of their material was lost. Although warned of the likelihood of sudden flooding, the foreman insisted on placing his hut close to the water's edge, only to see it floating away shortly after.

Flash floods were commonplace prior to the restoration of the Avon in the 1950s and on many occasions the water rose above the arches of the bridge, spilling across the road and surrounding fields, bringing with it a dangerous fast-flowing swell. On one sad occasion the choirboy son of Mr and Mrs Mumford, caretakers at Heathlands, fell into the swirling waters and was drowned.

The floods, photographed in the early 1930s. Jack Heeks (consort to Betty Hughes when she was Mayor of Pershore in 1991-92) stands watching as traffic slowly crosses the bridge. Just visible to the right, hard against the wall, is a raised walkway, known locally as the 'Duck Walk', which was erected to enable pedestrians to pass above the flood water.

On the road into town, Wisteria Cottage was aptly named. By 1925 the building was almost completely covered while metal railings had replaced the wooden fence. The next cottage is the old Toll House which today bears the plaque stating 'First District of Evesham Turnpike Trust – 1743-1877'. The house itself was not built until 1857 (costing £100), its site having been purchased by the Trustees from the Dean and Chapter of Westminster for a nominal consideration of £5. Early maps (from 1743) show a nearby toll bar. This was later moved the short distance to the position it now holds. The right to exact tolls was usually granted to the highest bidder at an annual public auction with the proviso that correct accounts be kept for inspection by the Magistrates and that the road and bridge be maintained in good order. A plaque attached to the same spot occupied by the original toll board records that the charge for vehicles drawn by six or more horses was 1/6. Soldiers on the march, all things employed in husbandry or manuring and anyone travelling to Sunday worship had free passage.

Entering the town by river one saw the Manor House Hotel and Partridge's Old Mill.

Stanhope House, built in 1760 by George Perrott for a nephew. The photograph shows the house in its entirety including the adjacent building (now the Ley School) and many outbuildings behind – pig sties, fowl houses, etc. The sideways portion was built as a chauffeur's flat with alongside, housed in the low building, the dairy and still rooms. Ley School and its outbuildings were split from the main house in 1934 when bought by Dr and Mrs Fleming.

The panelled study at Stanhope House, showing its Adam-style fireplace, 1934.

14

Many of the houses in Bridge Street were originally Elizabethan with Georgian frontages added later. No 26 is a good example. This 1960s photograph shows its original features at the rear where both upstairs and downstairs are half-timbered.

The Georgian influence is evident in this 1960s view of the pine-panelled parlour on the ground floor at the front of No 26 Bridge Street. Note the heads of the monarchs William and Mary above the chimney piece.

Perrott House, considered the finest building in Pershore, was built by George Perrott around 1770. He was a London lawyer who purchased the Lower Avon Navigation Rights, taking silk (i.e. becoming a King's Counsel) in 1759 and becoming a Judge four years later. Originally called Riverdale, the house was intended primarily as a house for entertaining, but Judge Perrott lived there in retirement from 1775 until his death in 1780. The antiques shop shown alongside, now Coach House Books, was the original coach house. To the right is Western House with further down the Star and Brandy Cask hotels.

The main hall of Perrott House, looking towards the garden door, 1960s.

Looking along Bridge Street towards High Street. On the left is Perrott House with, next-door, Western House, which was also built by George Perrott, on this occasion for his solicitor. Just visible is No 21 which in 1905 was occupied by a Mr R. Mills, plumber and painter. Due to the angle from which the photograph is taken, the houses on the left are difficult to number, although the castellated bay window of Carlton House (No 20) can be seen.

The top end of Bridge Street, early 1960. The barrels of the Three Tuns were later removed since lorries found difficulty in turning here without causing damage to the portico. This was solved by extending the pavement. The veranda opposite fronts Bedford House. Following an accident in which their son drowned, the Bedford family became keen supporters of the Royal National Lifeboat Institution donating the money to pay for several lifeboats. The buildings between Bedford House and the bow-fronted window (then Fearnside's) were demolished around 1966 and a new frontage erected. On this site stood a three-storey Elizabethan building, at one time the Black Swan, which was demolished when the alterations took place.

Broad Street before car parking! Until their demolition in 1836-37, six houses stood at the eastern end of the street. At the western end stands Myrtle Cottage (known for its flush toilets) where in 1905 lived Mrs Feek who always wore a lace skull cap and long skirts. Her husband Percy had a large collection of clocks and was a well-known local antiquarian. The entrance to Ganderton Yard was to the left of the three gabled houses.

A dancing demonstration in Broad Street in the early 1950s. Flags are out and dancers are wearing Western costume. It may well be that the event was part of Coronation celebrations when the whole country seemed to go 'square-dance crazy' following press photographs of the Queen and Prince Philip doing a dosi-do.

Ganderton Row (sometimes called Ganderton Yard) facing Broad Street. At one time there were seventeen occupied 'one up-one down' cottages with 32 children living there. The upstairs room was reached by a ladder through a small gap in the ceiling, as were houses in Reddings Yard (Church Street) and Bull Entry (Newlands). Ganderton Row was demolished in 1938.

The gate to Abbey House, later the Monastery. It was this wall over which the monks would lean, teasing children as they passed. They would also sit on the wall in the evenings reading by the light from the gas lamp opposite. In earlier times the gate to the left was the entrance to the flower show. St Andrew's churchyard was at this time railed off – in the past there had been complaints that loose animals were causing damage there.

Mrs Nan Howes standing at the doorway of No 12 Church Street, c. 1905. At the far end Mr Roberts opened a fish shop, later moving to No 9 on the opposite side of the road, next to the Vicarage. Later moves took the family to No 1 (which was purchased for £100), to the High Street, and then back to Church Street. The house adjoining the White Hart at the far end was later demolished as were the cottages in Reddings Yard.

Reddings Yard was a turning near the top end of Church Street, with two facing rows of 'one up-one down' cottages. At the bottom of the alley was an open washhouse area and communal toilets. To the right of the photograph was Saddlers' Yard behind which was a water pump serving the whole street.

An underground stream is thought to run from the Abbey Garage area and by Orchard Ditch. This compounded the many floods which occurred over the years. Here we see those in Priest Lane caused by a torrential storm in 1921. Bill and Kate Horton occupied the small shop on the corner (still existing). Mrs Horton had the sole rights to the sale of Sunday papers and would deliver them to the surrounding villages. The Engine Terrace cottages, on a site where the Health Centre now stands, were demolished in the early 1970s. The WI Hall, now the Judo Club, can just be seen behind the telegraph pole.

An earlier flood (1903) in the same area, showing Church Row and the Black Horse facing the Abbey. In the distance the tall wall surrounding Abbey House is just visible.

Looking up Newlands towards Three Springs Road with the Almonry on the left, opposite which was Godfrey's coal yard where you could borrow a wheelbarrow to carry your $\frac{1}{4}$ cwt. of coal (cost $3\frac{1}{2}d$). The gabled house on the left was later demolished (see next picture) and where the bay window can be seen was J. Palfrey the baker.

This black-and-white Tudor cottage with its high, pitched Elizabethan gable was the last of its type in Pershore.

The Old Lodging House which stood on the corner of New Road and Newlands. Following its demolition the area was used as rag and bone yard by the Scarrat family who lived in a caravan on the site and stored a fairground roundabout there. The road to the left (opposite Head Street) was once known as Crow Pool Lane. It is believed that generations ago there was a pool in the area of the old school.

The top of Newlands opposite Amerie Court, looking towards the Abbey. The cottages on the right have long since gone, while on the left, where Roland Rutter Court now stands, was Brant's wood yard. From here he would deliver firewood to shops and individuals in the surrounding area.

An early photograph taken before the advent of the cinema and the alterations to the Angel Inn and Posting House. At this time the entrance to the inn was by a side entrance reached through the adjacent archway. Over the central window it says 'Inland Revenue Office' while above the entry it states 'Gough's Family Commercial Hotel'. Next-door is Harringtons, a ladies' outfitters, and Field's ironmongery shop, later taken over by Mr Brown. Between these two shops is the original portion of the Midland Bank (see page 34). Opposite, Vaughan's corner shop advertises sports, exhibitions and fireworks events.

In the late 1920s Mrs Amplett's coffee tavern became the Empire Cinema (later the Plaza) where Fanny Hart and Arthur Priest accompanied the silent films. With the arrival of the 'talkies' the place was refurbished and toilets added behind, reached through a side entrance. In the mid-1930s the manager was Mr Marshall, an Australian. Both he and his wife (as usherette) wore full evening dress for their duties. The cinema played an important part in the life of the town with other special events taking place. In the 1950s the flourishing Pershore Dramatic Society would perform there for a three-day run which necessitated moving the seats and screen.

Once the home of Dr H.B. Emerson, this building was taken over by Pershore Rural District Council (RDC) in August 1938. The clock erected by the Town Council is a replacement for one purchased through a War Memorial Fund and installed on 18 October 1953 in memory of those who gave their lives in the Second World War and also to commemorate the Silver Jubilee of HM Queen Elizabeth II. Next-door is Lincoln House, now a dental practice. In the past this building was a select lodging house where only bank clerks or school teachers were welcomed.

The Redlands flats in the process of construction. Several houses, including the double-fronted Pomona House, were demolished to form the Cherry Orchard access. The gasometers were a prominent landmark until 1986. They were erected by the Pershore & District Gaslight Company and were reached through an opening in Sunnyside. This company went into liquidation in 1947 and its business was taken over by the Cheltenham & District Gas Co. until British Gas was formed by nationalisation of the industry.

High Street, at the turn of the century. The first of the flower-decked shops on the left was that of David Pardoe, a saddler, later Newell's (known as 'Tacky') the builders. Next-door was William Wood, fly proprietor, who sold and hired out carts and coaches of all types. The tall house was where the Phillips family lived and had their provision stores (see page 43). Behind the railing to the right is the Working Men's Club (see page 80) believed to be on the site of the Temperance Hall which was used by a large number of organisations in the town, amongst them the Mechanics Institute founded in 1849.

The storm on 14 June 1921 which caused floods in Priest Lane also affected the High Street. This photograph taken from an almost identical spot to that above shows the effect on houses and traffic.

The entrance to the Civic Centre is where this thatched cottage stood, *c.* 1905, while the cottages next to Woodlands have been replaced by flower beds. Opposite is the old Police Station, recently converted into apartments, where there were two cells and a stable in 1910, presided over by Inspector S. Davis. Alongside Head Street is The Vineyards, an Abbeyfields Society home, but originally an ale and beer house known as The Sign of the Zebra. During extensions at Central Garage opposite, human remains were found, thought to be from an old Quaker burial ground. The Quakers were very active in the area during the 1660s, with visits from George Fox, the founder of the movement.

A snowy scene where Station Road joins the Worcester Road showing Mercy Green's Cottage, *c.* 1905.

The junction of Station Road and Worcester Road. The railed triangle in the centre was removed in an attempt to make the area less dangerous when the junction became busier. In 1991 traffic lights were installed. The black-and-white cottages opposite are believed to have been built in the 1620s and at the time this photograph was taken one was occupied by 'Kelly' Bickerstaff.

Pershore Hall, also called The Mount, which was built by Edward Humphries. Several gardeners were employed, with Mr Dufty in charge of the greenhouses. There was also a tennis court and pool, with farmland and orchards behind. By 1908 William Deakin had taken over the property, growing fruit for his jam factories at Wigan and Farrington. Many of the local ladies earned money picking fruit – a blind eye often being turned by the manager as they tucked some into their bloomers for home consumption! Following the Second World War the building was converted into flats for Atlas Works employees.

Two

Shops, Ale and Public Houses

The life of Pershore has long been associated with its position on a main highway and with retailing. Although the Domesday Book does not mention a market, a coin from the reign of Edward the Confessor has been attributed to Pershore and since only market towns could mint such coins it is thought that this indicates a market here from at least the early 11th century. Usually held in Broad Street, the day of the market changed from Sunday to Tuesday in 1219. Seven years later, Henry III gave the Abbot of Pershore sole rights to hold a three-day Midsummer fair to celebrate the Feast of St Edburga. Additional fairs took place on Easter Tuesday, the first Monday in August, and the last Tuesday in October. Another fair, for the hiring of servants, took place on the Wednesdays before and after 11 October. The old weekly market ceased in 1876. Pershore has been well served by coaching inns, public beer and cider houses – at one time there were over thirty and the town gained a local reputation for indulging in drunkenness. Many of the pubs were associated with particular trades. By the 19th century several trades were carried on: stocking making, wool stapling and malting. Watch and clock springs were made and highly regarded, as was the work undertaken by women making up gloves. The Atlas Works, meanwhile, was becoming famous from about 1840 and there were two jam factories and a cider and mineral water factory.

The Three Tuns, on the corner of Bridge Street and Broad Street, c. 1910.

In 1868 Manor House Hotel was a private residence belonging to Dr William MacKensie. During the Second World War it became a Boys' School with German POWs working the gardens. Bought by Mr Bridges in 1945, it was run as a hotel from 1947 and a restaurant was built on the site of the vast Victorian conservatory which ran the length of the Manor. A bar upstairs was for club members' use only. It is said the top floor is haunted by a maid, complete with mob-cap and untidy hair. At the foot of the car park is an earthen mound. This covers the old ice-house. Such constructions allowed the discerning hostess to offer guests chilled wine and fancy desserts. During the 18th century, more than 3,000 ice-houses were installed in this country. Ice was collected during the winter, smashed into fragments and packed into a deep brick or stone-lined well, tapering at the bottom, domed at the top, with a drain allowing melt water to escape. There was another ice-house near Orchard Ditch at the edge of the Abbey grounds, probably belonging to Abbey House. This was fast deteriorating in the 1920s and no trace now remains.

An ice-house plan.

Crookes Brothers, family grocers and tea dealers at No 40 Bridge Street, *c.* 1900. The gentleman with the bicycle is Mr Henry Crooke (known as 'Ping-pong' Crooke) who was for some years a reporter for the *Evesham Journal* and a close friend of Edward Elgar. By the 1930s the right-hand side of the shop was closed and was being used as the Midlands Area headquarters of the British Union of Fascists by William Joyce (Lord Haw-Haw) then lodging at Wick (see page 128). At this time Nell Andrews kept a dairy on the left with a bakehouse to the rear.

The Brandy Cask Brewery, 1996, which is situated behind the Brandy Cask public house (originally a warehouse sending wool to Avonmouth via the river for export). Mr Alan Clayton is continuing a long-established Pershore occupation by brewing a selection of real ales. Having started in June 1995, he now brews $4\frac{1}{4}$ barrels (153 gallons) at each brew length, which he is able to undertake six or seven times a month.

The majority of the houses on the river side of Bridge Street have gardens fronting the water. The Star Hotel, originally the Coach and Horses owned by the Manor of Binholme, had a thriving business storing and renting out boats to tourists who would row to Wyre Mill and back. As a coaching inn it had stabling for ninety horses.

Willow Café managed by Lottie Spiers, daughter of Joseph Spiers the basket maker, No 1 Bridge Street, early 1950s.

The banks in Pershore own and care for some of the town's most beautiful buildings. Their Georgian doorways often show very lovely and intricate fanlights and that of Barclays Bank, pictured here, is amongst the finest.

As can be seen on page 24, Midland Bank (earlier known as the London Joint City and Midland Bank) originally occupied only the right-hand side of the building with a ladies outfitters to the left. This picture shows the bank in the early 1960s following the rebuilding of the first and second storeys. This work was necessary because of the porosity of the original bricks. Great care went into obtaining special materials to enable the new frontage to remain faithful to the original.

Shops on the right-hand side of Bridge Street, looking towards High Street, 1996. May Graham (previously Miss Winwood, fruit and veg) sold ladies' clothes. At Newick's they also sold fruit and vegetables, with groceries and cakes at R.J. Haines, who took over from Jinny Salmon (his wife's aunt, from 1948 until 1972). No 16 was the original post office, where mail bags hung from hooks in the ceiling, before becoming Fuller's shoe repairers. Next-door was Elkington the butcher which had a slaughterhouse at the rear. Then came Joseph Glover's, photographer.

The Three Tuns Hotel (see page 29) was one of the main coaching inns on the London to Worcester route along with the Angel, Coach & Horses, Bell and Kings Head. The prefix 'Royal' was added following a short stay by the Princess Victoria with her mother, the Duchess of Kent, on their way to Malvern in 1830. This 1960s picture shows the dining room situated above the portico. Alongside was a large ballroom with windows opening to the veranda. Grand balls were held here and it was also the meeting place for many types of organisations. An omnibus owned by the hotel would meet trains on request and even collected folk from home.

In 1983 the Three Tuns Hotel was purchased for development and was sympathetically transformed by Chartermart Property Investment Ltd of Ascot into eight shops, three offices and a restaurant. The original outer walls and portico were retained around a central courtyard and the development named the Royal Arcade.

Littleton & Badsey Growers Ltd shop in Broad Street, 1966. Selling various fertilisers and requisites to the horticultural industry, the Pershore shop was one of three owned by this firm which still exists at Littleton. It occupied the space created by the disappearance of Ganderton Yard but ceased trading on the building of sheltered accommodation a decade ago when the shop was incorporated in the new development.

Lloyds Bank, Broad Street. In 1905 the manager was Walter Pace, followed in 1908 by Charles Hunt. In 1918 the Capital & Counties Bank, long established in High Street, merged with Lloyds. In 1930, when the manager was Thomas Sheaf, the bank moved to new premises in Broad Street. At this time banking rules regarding staff dress and behaviour were extremely strict. During the Second World War Bill Pugh the then manager was a well-loved character – he once entered the Carnival … as a carnival queen! He was also noted for his loud snore which, it was said, could be heard from the street.

Prothero's corner shop advertised itself in this fashion in the 1910 issue of the *Pershore Almanac.*

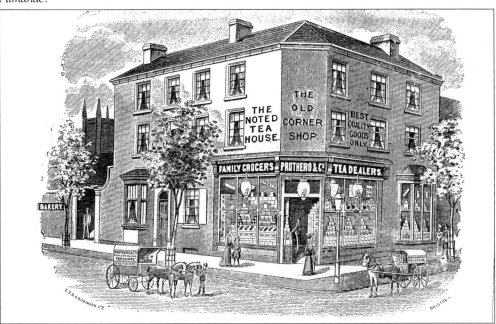

The corner shop at the junction of Broad Street and High Street had a series of owners, from Vaughan's (page 24) to Prothero's (page 37). Like many local shops they kept open as long as customers called. They baked their own bread in a bakery adjoining the Broad Street side of the shop and delivered to villages. Later owners were Burtons (pictured above in the 1940s) and Fine Fare (below, early 1970s) before the premises were taken as an estate agent's. The two ailing trees in High Street unaccountably died in spite of being copiously watered by Mrs Roberts who owned the fish and chip shop next to the Co-op.

The Angel Inn and Posting House is another of the original coaching inns where vehicles travelling between London and Holyhead changed horses. There was stabling and extensive grounds behind the building. The picture shows the bar in an upstairs room decorated for a dance, with John Pettifer, Ray Till, Mary ?, and Sylvia Jones. The theme for the evening was Bruce Bairnsfather's 'If you know of a better 'ole, go to it' – a well-known cartoon from the First World War.

A 1958 menu from the Angel Inn when a three-course meal cost seven shillings with coffee 6d extra. On the reverse side a recipe for lemon marmalade is given. In support of the surmise that 'Queen Elizabeth slept here' a portrait of Queen Elizabeth I was revealed on a wall when alterations were made in 1922. At that time there were four live-in staff – a housekeeper, barmaid, waitress and chambermaid, – with a daily cook, general handyman and charlady.

The Angel Inn & Posting House
Pershore

Luncheon 7/-
12.30.....1.45.

Date August 7th 1958.

MENU

Spring Vegetable Soup
Fruit or Tomato Juice

Fried Fillet of Plaice - Tartare Sauce
Fried Dover Sole - Lemon
Grilled Lamb Cutlet - Mint Sauce
Meat Curry - Rice - Chutney
Grilled Ham - Egg
Cold Boiled Ham - Salad

New Potatoes   Chipped Potatoes
Kidney Beans

Bakewell Tart & Custard
Creamed Semolina Pudding
Strawberry / Vanilla or Chocolate Ice Cream
Biscuits & Cheese
-- -------

Coffee 6d.

F. Greenhous, ironmonger, 1905. Mr Greenhous was related to the motor-car people at Shrewsbury and Hereford. He sold all manner of hardware goods, including bicycles and an abundance of 'Stick-tite', a tree-bonding compound.

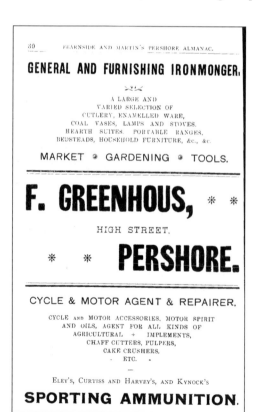

GENERAL AND FURNISHING IRONMONGER,

A LARGE AND
VARIED SELECTION OF
CUTLERY, ENAMELLED WARE,
COAL VASES, LAMPS AND STOVES,
HEARTH SUITES, PORTABLE RANGES,
BEDSTEADS, HOUSEHOLD FURNITURE, &c., &c.

MARKET ● GARDENING ● TOOLS.

F. GREENHOUS, ✳ ✳

HIGH STREET,

✳ ✳ **PERSHORE.**

CYCLE & MOTOR AGENT & REPAIRER.

CYCLE AND MOTOR ACCESSORIES, MOTOR SPIRIT
AND OILS, AGENT FOR ALL KINDS OF
AGRICULTURAL + IMPLEMENTS,
CHAFF CUTTERS, PULPERS,
CAKE CRUSHERS,
. ETC. -

ELEY'S, CURTISS AND HARVEY'S, AND KYNOCK'S

SPORTING AMMUNITION.

An advertisement which appeared in the 1910 edition of the *Pershore Almanac*.

In 1945 the Greenhous ironmongery became the premises of the Co-operative Society with tastefully installed, curved bay windows. Still later the building underwent further modernisation and ugly side windows were inserted and a side entrance. The Co-op, which had already opened a store in September 1927 on the corner of Priest Lane and High Street, actually purchased the lower premises in 1953, when the store was converted from non-food to a grocery and the Priest Lane premises was closed.

Another 'modernisation' – the windows of St George's dry cleaners, now Wanderers World. Two doors away, the building with the window topped by a circle was owned by Mr Bruff, an agricultural engineer, known as 'The Man on the Spot', hence the logo. After his death, the firm was taken over by Nick Strickland whose firm has progressed steadily to become known the world over.

By 1905 the International Stores was well established under manager Jim Alan, second from the left. The other staff are: Joe Winkett, Albert Young, Danny Hill, Nellie Foster, Bill Smith and Frank Checketts, who was sadly killed during the Second World War. This was the site of the Bell Hotel, another coaching inn which boasted a first-floor ballroom with gold-painted rafters.

Harry Watts owned a coach-building business in the yard behind the International. He manufactured market gardener's drays until, with the introduction of motor cars, the demand failed. John Annis's father worked here as a painter when the firm was in demand for decorating both carriages and boats, among them those for Lord Coventry. The building later became a series of lock-up garages, until destroyed by fire in the 1980s.

No 66 High Street. This grocery and bakery shop was purchased from the Co-op Wholesale Society by George Phillips in the 1860s and had in its back yard the old music hall, a stable (later demolished) and a bakery, where people brought their Christmas roasts for cooking. The baker during the 1920s was Jules Hart, a Frenchman, who made unusual confectionery to complement the more traditional cakes make by Mr Phillips's mother. The shop adjacent to the entry was also owned by the Phillips family, as was the three-storey building itself, where the family lived and had its offices. The family later acquired No 42 High Street (pictured below, later Wakefield's the butcher), together with the shop on the corner of Church Street, then worked by Mr Kettel, a saddler.

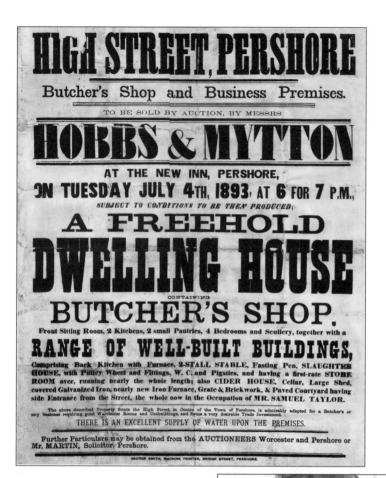

HIGH STREET, PERSHORE

Butcher's Shop and Business Premises.

TO BE SOLD BY AUCTION, BY MESSRS

HOBBS & MYTTON

AT THE NEW INN, PERSHORE,

ON TUESDAY JULY 4TH, 1893, AT 6 FOR 7 P.M.,

SUBJECT TO CONDITIONS TO BE THEN PRODUCED;

A FREEHOLD

DWELLING HOUSE

CONTAINING

BUTCHER'S SHOP,

Front Sitting Room, 2 Kitchens, 2 small Pantries, 4 Bedrooms and Scullery, together with a

RANGE OF WELL-BUILT BUILDINGS,

Comprising Back Kitchen with Furnace, 2-STALL STABLE, Fasting Pen, SLAUGHTER HOUSE, with Pulley Wheel and Fittings, W. C. and Pigsties, and having a first-rate STORE ROOM over, running nearly the whole length; also CIDER HOUSE, Cellar, Large Shed, covered Galvanized Iron, nearly new Iron Furnace, Grate & Brickwork, & Paved Courtyard having side Entrance from the Street, the whole now in the Occupation of MR. SAMUEL TAYLOR.

The above described Property fronts the High Street, in Centre of the Town of Pershore, is admirably adapted for a Butcher's or any business requiring good Warehouse Rooms and Outbuildings, and forms a very desirable Trade Investment.

THERE IS AN EXCELLENT SUPPLY OF WATER UPON THE PREMISES.

Further Particulars may be obtained from the AUCTIONEERS Worcester and Pershore or Mr. MARTIN, Solicitor, Pershore.

GEORGE SMITH, MACHINE PRINTER, BRIDGE STREET, PERSHORE.

The central building was originally The Swan, formerly The Quiet Woman and situated next to the 'new' post office. The earlier post office was situated in Bridge Street and even though deliveries then arrived by bicycle there were still four each day, with much of the post within the town arriving the same day it was posted. There was even a collection and delivery each Sunday with the office open during the morning for the purchase of stamps and for registration of letters. Before the gas shop took over the renovated building, Mr Willis, lamb butcher, occupied the premises.

44

This building at the top end of the town was a public house until 1915. Although the white background has disappeared, the slogan 'Celebrated Ales & Guinness' is still visible on the walls either side of this now private house. Cyclists were welcomed and accommodation and teas provided. In 1891 William Featherstone, the then landlord, was charged with unlawfully keeping open house until 1 o'clock on the morning of 15 January and was fined ten shillings plus expenses. In 1930 the building was a cobbler's shop under the management of G. Teale.

The Plough Inn, 1906. In 1745 this was a thatched cottage occupied by Mary, said to haunt the building wearing a striped dress. Inquests were often held here. One took place on 27 March 1851 on John Hemming, currier, aged 72, for allowing a house of questionable repute. Next-door was the Crown & Anchor which became a private house in 1884. From here Mr Clemens ran a coal business. His son, interested in constructing radios, scoured Bredon Hill for the crystals used and in 1922 he entered partnership with Arthur Taylor to make radios. Thus was born Wireless Supply.

Originally a thatched building, the White Horse was demolished in the late 19th century and the present three-storey structure built in its place. There was much concern by the then Vicar that the greater height of the new building would enable folk to see over the Vicarage wall and so he added a further three feet to the height of the latter! As can be seen from the picture, the White Horse had its own brewery. Nearby in Church Street, where the library now stands, was the Butchers Arms. It was the landlord here – George Crooks – who in 1833 discovered the wild plums growing in Tiddesley Woods, from which the Pershore Egg variety was developed.

The Black Horse at the corner of Priest Lane and Church Row. An inn before 1745, Jane Stoker was its landlord in 1895. It continued as an ale house until 29 November 1967.

Newlands at the junction with New Road and Head Street. The corner house, recently converted into apartments was Palfrey's and Harding's shop and bakery. Next-door was a grocer's shop, with the Talbot public house alongside. This was called the Waterloo Tavern in 1855 and it is likely that both Royalists and Roundheads were accommodated there during the Civil War since Newlands was at that time part of a main road. It is said that the ghost of a Royalist soldier has been seen at the rear of the building.

This shop with its liberal embellishment of adverts for various teas, cigarettes and Windowlene was owned by Mrs Pritchard and stood at the lower end of Newlands near the access to Little Priest Lane. This was originally yet another public house – The White Hart.

VE Day celebrations in the yard of the Victoria Hotel, 1945. This hotel is situated at the corner of Newlands and Head Street, a plastered wall concealing the original red brick. A one-time landlord here was Mr Butt, a skipper of the *Pisgah*.

Mrs Bick kept a butcher's shop next to the old lock-up in Newlands. She sometimes used to store her meat there saying it was as cold as any ice-box. Known as the sheep-stealers' prison, drunkards were also confined there and it is said that when it was demolished its lower walls were impregnated with urine as a consequence. There was a further lock-up behind No 10 Bridge Street where there were two cells. One of its old doors is now to be seen in the Heritage Centre at No 5 Bridge Street.

The Coventry Arms Hotel was built some hundred years ago by the 9th Earl of Coventry, in connection, it is thought, with the Croome Estate jam factory (built 1889). This latter business was later acquired by T.W. Beach & Sons Ltd. The hotel was the focus of much village life with many activities taking place there. The picture shows residents about to embark on a trip to Madresfield on 5 August 1920 in a charabanc probably supplied by C.C. George of Pershore. In 1910 the landlord was Mr Bosley.

Posted in 1906, this postcard shows the railway station, looking towards Worcester, with station-master Henry Jakeways, who in 1908 won a third prize for the best and neatest-kept Great Western station garden. Served by the Great Western Railway, the station boasted an attractive booking office and waiting room. Passengers travelling towards London needed to cross the footbridge which was built in 1901.

Aerial view of Pershore, taken by Adrian Summerton, early 1970s.

Three
Church and Chapel

Pershore's Abbey was one of the earliest Christian foundations in Worcestershire. It is generally accepted that by 689 a community existed here although earlier dates have been suggested. At one time the foundation was very wealthy with extended possessions but its strength had diminished greatly by the 16th century and in 1539 only 14 monks were left. The Reformation and the dissolution of the monasteries forced the surrender of Pershore Abbey to the king and its outbuildings were demolished and the church lost its nave and lady chapel.

In the 1800s the fabric of the remaining Abbey was in poor condition but a vast restoration scheme was undertaken at the instigation of Rev Williamson (1850-65) and the Lantern Tower was opened up. In 1913 two buttresses were added on the west side, with a vestry added in 1936. The official millennium of the Abbey was celebrated in 1972 and urgent repair work has been necessary recently.

Pershore Abbey, seen from the north-west, *c.* 1865, with St Andrew's Church to the east. This early photograph clearly shows the roof line of the original north transept and a tiny blocked access door to the roof. It also shows the Abbey before the pinnacles were added in 1871. It is said that the needlewomen of Pershore were so highly regarded by glove makers in Worcester that they wished to show their appreciation by paying for a spire to be added to the tower. However, it proved to be unsuitable and pinnacles were added instead.

Pershore Abbey and St. Andrews

The close proximity of two churches – the Abbey and St Andrew's Church – often perplexes visitors . The explanation lies in the fact that past ownership of the town was divided between Pershore Abbey and Westminster. This division continued beyond the Reformation when the town was two distinct parishes – that of St Andrew's and Holy Cross. These two parishes remained independent until their merger in 1949. In 1840 Rev D'Arcy Haggitt was Vicar of St Andrew's with Rev Palmer and Rev Foley, curates. It sat 632 with services at 11am and Sunday school meetings held at the National School.

The interior of Holy Cross as it was at the turn of the century when the altar was set at the rear of the 1816 sanctuary built on the site of the Chapel of Our Lady. The altar of the early Abbey church would have been just outside the present west door – at the end of the original nave which consisted of ten bays about 180 feet long and 60ft wide. The entrance to this is presently marked by metal gates.

Looking from the Lantern Tower in the early 1960s towards the then newly installed free-standing altar. On the altar steps are communion kneelers specially designed for the Abbey and depicting fruit grown in the surrounding district. They were worked by a number of local needlewomen.

A split-view postcard showing five different aspects of the Abbey. The Norman font was replaced during Victorian times and a new one set in the south transept. The whereabouts of the original was unknown for many years. However, it was eventually discovered acting as a flower container in the garden of The Nash at Kempsey, whence it was returned to the Abbey. The Victorian replacement was sent to a church in Ceylon.

Pershore's war memorial, erected in the south transept (the oldest part of the Abbey) and associated with monuments from earlier wars. Sir Aston Webb recommended Alfred Drury RA as designer and sculptor. His design featured the figure of Immortality holding an olive branch of peace in her left hand, bestowing the crown of everlasting life with the other. She stands on a Portland stone pedestal which bears a bronze plaque depicting a fallen soldier with an angel at his head and his widow and child at the foot. The monument was constructed by Messrs Collins and Godfrey of Tewkesbury at a cost of £927. It was dedicated on 1 November 1921 and unveiled by the Earl of Coventry, Lord Lieutenant of the County.

Monks fishing in the pond at Abbey House. In 1914 a group of Anglican monks from the Caldey Island community in Pembrokeshire, who had remained faithful to the Church of England when the rest of the community joined the Roman Catholic Church, settled at Abbey House to the south-west of the Abbey. Within 12 years this group had grown so large that the house was too small to accommodate them and they moved in 1926 to Nashdom in Buckinghamshire.

The rear of the almonry as it appeared in the 1960s having remained derelict for some years. This building stands on the site of the monastic almonry, used by visitors to the monastery and for the distribution of alms to the poor. Almost certainly dating from the early 17th century, some of the beams are said to have come from part of the Abbey demolished at the dissolution in 1540. A plaque on the wall today commemorates the restoration of this building in 1973 by the Worcestershire Building Conservation Trust. A view of the front of the house as it was early in the century appears on page 22.

Pershore Abbey choir at the beginning of this century. In the back row, second from the left, is Arthur Hall, who was killed during the First World War. First on the right in the third row is Albert Harry Annis.

The Abbey Choir, c. 1924, with William Needs, verger, and Charles Mason, organist and choirmaster standing next to the bishop. Others are thought to be Mrs Slater, Duncan Gibbs and William Smith.

Mothers Union at Avonbank, 7 September 1911.

Sunday school whist drive, 23 December 1911.

Nativity play performed by members of the Abbey congregation in the 1930s.

Friends of the Abbey service, 1936. The organisation founded by Dr W.T. Farncombe, seen here standing next to the Judge, held its first festival on 29 June 1930 with special services and an outdoor procession of robed clergy. John Masefield, the then Poet Laureate, read some of his own poems. Rev Brigham, the curate who was killed in the Second World War, is seen in the back row.

At the invitation of Pershore Festival Committee, members from a well-dressing society in Derbyshire set up one of their traditional well-head displays portraying the Abbey. Set into large trays of clay, the pictures are made up from thousands of flower petals and leaves. In the picture is the then Vicar, Rev Peter Moore with Bishop Charles Edwards.

In 1552 the Abbey housed five bells, thought to have been made in the 1480s. Today there are eight, six cast by Gloucester bellmaker Abraham Rudhall in 1729. A small 1 cwt. bell inscribed 'Haste Away, Make No Delay' was stolen during the 1863 restorations. During the 1996 excavations a bell-casting pit – as yet undated – was located in the south transept. The carillon, which plays every three hours from 9am to 9pm, was installed in 1879. St Andrew's bells are even older: six date from 1715, with two from 1982 when the originals were taken to Loughborough for re-tuning as the picture shows. Both sets of bells are justly famous and attract ringers from all over the country.

In 1848 the then Vicar pulled down the old Vicarage soon after his appointment and built the present building – a much larger one – through the assistance of a loan from the Queen Anne's Fund, repayable by instalment. Unfortunately, after various extravagances, he became so deeply in debt that his creditors sequestrated the living. He left the parish and was later confined to a lunatic asylum in Bruges.

The Monastery, also known as Abbey House, stood on the site of Abbey buildings adjoining the western side of the cloister. Built about 1830 by the Bedford family, it later became home to the Scobell family before being occupied for twelve years after 1910 by a Benedictine community. It was demolished during the 1930s and the site is now occupied by today's bowling club. The club, formed in 1928, sprang from an invitation by the Lord Abbot, the first President of the club, to tradesmen of the town to play bowls on the Monastery lawn. The club began with two rinks until Pershore RDC took over the surrounding grazing and market garden land for housing, retaining an area as park land (Abbey Park).

St Andrew's Church was founded, probably at the time of Edward the Confessor, to accommodate the tenants of Westminster, for there was much bitterness between them and the monks of Pershore due to the large amount of Pershore property being made over to Westminster. The church was originally a gift of the Prior and monks of Malvern but in 1241 it was granted to the Monastery. It has been restored and rebuilt at various times but the present structure is chiefly 15th-century. In 1971 the disused church and its grounds were converted into a parish centre under the leadership of Canon Christopher Campling.

The earliest part of the building is the north arcade and west wall dating from the 12th century. The church had a chancel of $26\frac{1}{2}$ft x 17ft, nave, north and south aisles. Today, one enters through the original south porch with the south aisle (42ft x 21ft) converted into the entrance, committee room and kitchen. The three-stage 12ft-square tower has a ground floor converted into toilets and stairs leading to a second stage from which bells are now rung, finally leading into an upper storey above the kitchen complex. The original nave (51ft x 12ft) led into the chancel which was where the raised area is now partitioned from the main social area, with a vestry on the left-hand side.

61

There is evidence of four medieval crosses in Pershore: the High Cross, thought to have stood at the High Street end of Broad Street; Bowyers Cross, probably at the top end of High Street; Newlands Cross (site unknown) and Hampton Cross (probably near the bridges). Thus, there would have been one in the centre of town and one at each of the main entrances. While the remnant which now stands in the Abbey grounds is identical to a description given by an old inhabitant in 1865, this is said to have been moved from Wyre Piddle to the Abbey House grounds in 1844 where it stood when this picture was taken, probably being moved to its present position after the demolition of the house.

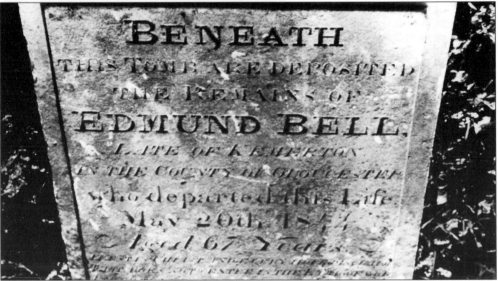

Edmund Bell, a sailor, was born in Ryde on the Isle of Wight. In 1825 he bought two Stuart cottages at Kemerton and converted them into a castle with battlements and observation posts. This later became the home of the Holland-Martins. It is believed Bell was a smuggler, carrying loot from pirated French ships by river from the Bristol Channel, in response to signals from his building and that there was a secret passage on the side of Bredon Hill where goods were hidden. Some say Bell was eventually executed for smuggling, others that he died in 1844 in Cheltenham Hospital. Either way, his body was given to the care of a niece who was able to have it buried in Pershore churchyard on payment of a fee to the Abbey monks. For some years this burial monument stood in a corner outside St Andrew's. Mrs Dufty, a well-known Pershore resident who died recently aged 103, was his granddaughter.

Mr James Ford and Captain Clayton of the Church Army. The Mission Hall, now known as St Agatha's and in the possession of the Town Council, was built in 1895 for the poor folk in the town who felt uncomfortable in the more affluent atmosphere of the Abbey. Behind the hall was an area available for sports and before the First World War there was a large gymnasium sited there where a parochial supper was held each January. This was apparently demolished during the Second World War.

Harvest festival decorations organised by the Church Army in the 1920s. Captain Clayton, its head, lived in Defford Road in the house which separated the boys from the girls' section of the National School.

Pershore Brotherhood pictured outside the Mission Hall, *c.* 1930.

Brotherhood Bowling Club, at the rear of the Mission Hall, 1936. Other sports were also held on this ground including steel quoits.

The Baptist church, one of the oldest in the country, is thought to have been founded in 1658. An early preacher was Richard Claridge, originally Rector of Peopleton who joined the Baptists in October 1691. At the end of the 17th century the minister was Timothy Thomas, under whom the Broad Street site of the chapel was secured in 1700. The present church dates from 1840 with a new manse built in 1868. In 1873 Julius Feek, father of the well-known antiquarian Percy Feek, began a 30-year pastorate here.

Interior of the Baptist church decorated for the Pershore Festival in the 1960s. In the foreground is the baptistry at the rear of the church. In the 1980s the church underwent modernisation at which time the pews were removed.

The Roman Catholic church in Priest Lane was founded in 1908 by Father Norman Holly, chaplain to the Berkeley family at Spetchley Park, first holding service in the Music Hall. Father Holly later acquired a tin hut (see picture below) from Mr Patten and in 1913 the Archbishop of Birmingham inaugurated a parish of about fifty members. Until 1928 the parish was run from Besford Court and until 1953 Pershore shared priests with Upton-upon-Severn. Thanks to a diocesan grant, the foundations of a purpose-built church were laid in May 1958 and the building was completed by Maundy Thursday 1959. The primary school and presbytery were built in 1967.

In November 1897 Princess Louise, a descendant of the last King of France and sister to the Duke of Orleans married Prince Charles, brother-in-law of the King of Spain. The wedding took place in a temporary chapel specially built at Wood Norton Hall which had been purchased by Duc d'Aumale as a home for the exiled French royal family. Although the ceremony was performed by the Bishop and Abbé before an august congregation, it was not considered legal by the Catholic authorities. Thus, just prior to the service, a secret ceremony took place at Evesham Catholic chapel, then in High Street. This chapel was later moved to Priest Lane where it was used for many years as a builder's store, as shown in the picture.

Four

Organisations
and Events

Pershore has always been a busy community with flourishing activities. Both national and local organisations were well supported and enthusiastically attended. Two years following the inception of the Scout movement there was a local troop and the Women's Institute in Pershore was one of the first in the country. In 1910 there were fourteen organisations meeting weekly, one fortnightly and five monthly, in addition to many horticultural and sports clubs. There were eight charities and a workhouse and cottage hospital caring for the poor and sick. Although it could not be considered a wealthy town, the community always banded together when necessary: doors remained unlocked, neighbours assisted each other and when funds were needed for good causes they seemed always to be forthcoming. For example, the then huge sum of £200,000 was collected during Warship Week in the Second World War. A more recent event has been the funding of the swimming pool. As long ago as 1910 the Coronation Committee decided on a swimming bath as a permanent memorial to the occasion but it was not until local people banded together that one was eventually opened in 1972.

Pershore Scout Troop, *c.* 1911, pictured in front of Park House, Elmley Castle.

Two years after the introduction of scouting by Robert Baden Powell in 1907, a troop was in existence at Pershore. An early supporter of the movement was General Sir Francis Davies, owner of Park House, Elmley Castle. Known locally as the 'Big House', this was demolished in 1963. As President of the Evesham district he allowed scout groups to meet in the deer park and on 8 May 1911 Lord Baden Powell himself inspected eight patrols and presented Pershore troop with its colours.

This picture shows a beacon built by the district boy scouts on Bredon Hill to celebrate the Silver Jubilee of King George V and Queen Mary in 1935. For many centuries the summit of the hill has been the site of such beacons as part of a country-wide system to warn of danger or celebrate great occasions.

Pershore Rovers Football Club, 1912, who played near Bearcroft (in the Orchard Ditch area). From left to right, back row: L. Dolphin (behind), A.H. Annis, W. Lock, T. Evans, P. Smith, Jack Young. Middle row: C. Milward, R.C. Edwards, A. Young. Front row: L. Twigg, T. Willis, H. Dyson, C. Turvey, G. Bozzard.

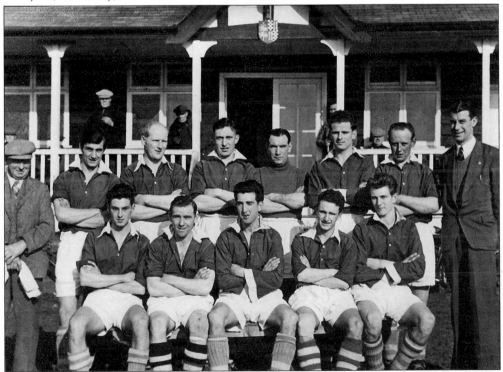

Pershore United Football Club, 1952-53 season. From left to right, back row: 'Kelly' Brant, Derek Garside, Bill Price, Victor Boulter, ? Attwood, Billy Ballinger. Front row: ? Attwood, Bill Taylor, Dennis Whittaker, -?-, 'Kitey' Wright.

The 1st Pershore Boys Brigade Company, 1915. This company, which was attached to the Abbey, was not in existence for many years.

Pershore Boys Life Brigade attached to the Baptist church. In 1910 the Captain was Mr W. Ballard and the Lieutenant, Mr G.H. Bloxsom.

Crowds attending a suffragette meeting outside the Hygienic Bakery in Broad Street, *c.* 1910. Miss Feek, daughter of Percy Feek, was one of the first supporters of the 'Votes for Women' campaign. It may be her who is seen here addressing the meeting.

In early Pershore almanacs, the Glee Society is recorded under the title of 'Mr Mason's Glee Society. Mr C. Mason was the conductor, and presumably the founder, of the group while the President was Rev F.R. Lawson. Rehearsals were held at St Agatha's Mission Hall every Tuesday at 9pm.

Pershore Operatic Musical Society in *Iolanthe*, 1911. The society was founded in 1902 by Miss Fanny Stephens of Bridge Street, its first director and conductor. From then until the outbreak of the First World War, the society performed a selection of Gilbert and Sullivan operettas: *Pirates of Penzance* (1909); *Patience* (1910); *Iolanthe* (1911); *The Mikado* (1912); *The Gondoliers* (1913), with a professional London coach employed for a week before each production at the Music Hall. Miss Stephens, a school teacher, also produced children's plays and pantomimes.

The Music Hall, 1997. Built by Worcester Co-operative Society in 1864 for £500, it was approached through an archway where Tolley's the jewellers now stands. The Phillips family, who owned the building storing barrels of cider and pickling vinegar in its cellars, were staunch supporters of the Arts and members of several musical societies – Joan Phillips becoming the founder of today's Pershore Choral Society. The hall was used for a vast variety of events: concerts, exhibitions, shows, meetings, etc., closing on 3 May 1862. Later, occasional events took place there but there is no record of any after 1920. In 1993 Pershore Operatic & Dramatic Society (founded 1989) took a five-year lease but at its completion developers plan to convert the building into flats.

At Pershore Flower Show 1909. No. 5

Pershore's Horticultural Society was founded in 1846 with a flower show organised in 1875. By 1896 it was advertised as 'one of the most comprehensive and best arranged in the Midlands', usually taking place in August. In addition to the flower, vegetable and craft competition, held in a large marquee, there was a promenade concert and horse jumping. Athletic sports also took place with a wooden stand built for spectators. The church bells rang, there were trips to the top of the Abbey tower, everyone wore their Sunday best and the whole event culminated with a large firework display.

Half-Mile Handicap. (Local) 1909.

On 28 May 1910 a Memorial Service and Parade commemorating the late King Edward VII was held which drew large crowds. The two pictures show members of the congregations turning into Broad Street following the Abbey service, and a portion of the parade.

Congregating in Broad Street for the Peace Day Parade, 16 August 1919. Henry Palfrey, whose cart can just be seen, was a baker and confectioner in High Street.

Prayer in thanksgiving for peace.

A PRAYER

for use in every home

At 12, noon, on

Sunday, 6th January, 1918.

" Our fathers hoped in Thee: they trusted in Thee, and Thou didst deliver them. They called upon Thee, and were holpen: they put their trust in Thee, and were not confounded.—Psalm xxii, 4, 5.

Prayer.

" O Almighty God, Who rulest in the kingdoms of men; hear, we beseech Thee, the prayers of our nation this day. We confess that we have done amiss, and dealt wickedly. Remember not our offences, nor the offences of our forefathers. Grant to us true repentance, forgiveness of our sins, and a steadfast purpose to serve Thee.

Deliver us from the great dangers which beset us, at home and abroad; giving to us both victory over our enemies, and peace among ourselves.

We thank Thee for the spirit of service shown by our sailors and soldiers, and by all who have borne with patience the burdens of these years of war.

Unite us, by Thy Holy Spirit, in love for one another, and in the earnest desire to do Thy holy will, that we may henceforth serve Thee in newness of life, through Jesus Christ our Lord. Amen."

" When they saw the star, they rejoiced with exceeding great joy."—St. Matthew ii., 10.

Epiphany, 1918.

The Peace Day Parade led by the band of the Worcestershire Regiment, turns along Broad Street from Bridge Street, passing what appears to have been a saluting rostrum.

Parade celebrating the Coronation of King George VI and Queen Elizabeth in 1937, proceeding up Bridge Street and past the Three Tuns.

Living bridge, 1922. Produced by Nancy Matthews, the head of Drakes Broughton School, some fifty people took part, acting out a game of bridge, appropriately dressed as the suits in a pack of cards. Ten years later the President of the Women's Institute organised 'Living whist' along the same lines, often with whole families taking part and small children playing the lower end of the suit. All cards shuffled round in the arena while music played and cards were chosen.

Crowds in Broad Street celebrating Empire Day, 1927. Behind the crowd is the entry to Nash's Passage and the house on the right was the telephone exchange.

PERSHORE EMERGENCY NEWS.

No. 4.   Registered as a Newspaper.   MONDAY, MAY 10th, 1926.   Price One Penny.

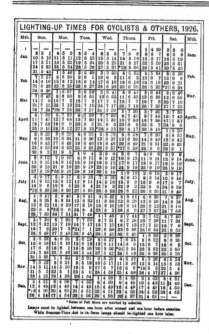

LIGHTING-UP TIMES FOR CYCLISTS & OTHERS, 1926.

Lamps must be lighted half-an-hour after sunset and one hour before sunrise.
While Summer-Time Act is in force lamps should be lighted one hour later.

BRIGHTER OUTLOOK.

MANY WORKERS RETURN.

RAILWAYS IMPROVING.

IRISH SHIPMENTS.

EDITORIAL.

A supply of *Birmingham Daily Post, Bristol Times and Mirror and Western Mail* are expected daily (commencing Monday about 12noon. Anyone wanting either of these papers **must place a regular** order for same. The papers will be delivered to customers in Pershore same day, but owing to late hour of arrival, delivery in surrounding villages cannot be made till day following publication.

The *Pershore Emergency News* will not continue to publish after a regular supply of daily papers is assured.

LATEST NEWS BY TELEGRAPH.

(Press Association).

Saturday.

Government Report.

Government spokesman stated to-day that general situation was much the same as yesterday. In London and home counties most of railways report improvements on yesterday's services, good progress is being made in handling of food stuffs at depots and sidings.

Road transports generally satisfactory and there has been no recurrence of interference with petrol depots. Post and mail services stated to be improving.

Miners' Report.

Mr. Cook reports no change. Miners executive met this afternoon in London. Mr. Cook informed press association that there had been absolutely no change in situation and that there were no signs at present of any peace moves.

Position has been considerably strengthened from men's point of view to-day and there was not likely to be any new phase in situation earlier than Monday.

T.U.C. stop Irish Shipments.

The general council of the British Trade Union Congress have intimated to the Irish Trade Unions that shipments from Ireland to British ports should stop for the present.

Communists Arrested.

A number of men, and one woman were remanded at Bradford to-day on charge of breach of emergency regulations order. Defendants were arrested following a visit by police officers to communists club at Gallows Hill, Shipley, on Wednesday.

Train held up.

Last night a passenger train on London and North Eastern Railway from Grimsby to Sheffield was held up for an hour by strikers at Worksop, men refused to move at level crossing until dispersed by police. There was no violence.

Improved Train Service.

Number of trains running yesterday were L.M.S. 760. L.N.E. 760. G.W.R.

GREAT FOOD CONVOY.

Escort of Armoured Cars and Cavalry.

Sunday.

London docks were opened yesterday by volunteers. Two battalions of Guards had taken possession overnight. About midday a great Food Convoy consisting of 104 lorries each with 3 or 4 soldiers in full kit including steel helmets, accompanied by armoured cars and cavalry passed right across London. There was no interference. It was received enthusiastically all along the route.

Electricity Workmen Back.

Men who had been on strike at Great Yarmouth Corporation Electricity Power Station, where volunteers had carried on, resumed work this morning.

Telegraph Wires Cut.

A number of telegraph wires between Newcastle and Hexham, on the railway, were discovered cut this morning. About twenty post offices were also cut off.

Further Riots in Glasgow.

There was a renewal last night of lively scenes in the east end of Glasgow, up to midnight. Forty-eight arrests had been made following baton charges.

Attack on Train.

Attack on Berwick to Newcastle corridor train was made at Killingworth crossing last night. Three or four hundred men bombarded the train with stones, one missile striking the stoker.

General Survey.

Last night's statement issued by general council Trades' Union Congress repeats statement that strike was an industrial struggle, and Council was not challenging constitution.

Northern Ireland.

The Ulster Government have issued a proclamation that a state of emergency exists in Northern Ireland.

Lord Oxford in a message to British Gazette regarding general strike says we should have lost all sense of self-respect if we were to allow any section of the community to bring to a stand-still the industrial and social life of the whole nation.

Government spokesman announced this evening there had been no serious disturbances in any part of the country, and food, light and power services had been successfully maintained.

The Archbishop of Canterbury after conference with representatives of the Free churches states they submit as basis possible—concordat return to status quo of Friday last.

The Government issued a statement yesterday afternoon, notifying all ranks of His Majesty's forces that full support would be given in any action taken in honest endeavour to aid civil power, both now and afterwards.

In disturbances at Hull yesterday afternoon, police made baton charges. Seven persons were injured.

A destroyer has arrived at Holyhead and landed a number of Naval ratings and

During the General Strike of 1926 many towns issued their own newsheets in the absence of official newspapers. In Pershore this was printed and published by W. Fearnside of Bridge Street.

Fancy dress helpers at Pershore fête in the 1920s.

Pershore Women's Institute (WI) was formed in 1916 with Mrs Geoffrey Hooper of The Croft the first President. Obtaining loans, she was able to purchase the WI hall erected in Priest Lane and there was soon a membership of over one hundred. During the Second World War the hall became a welfare centre and a canteen for servicemen was held nightly – one evening they served over 1,000! A canning machine was installed and great quantities of fruit and vegetables preserved. There was a flourishing drama group and choir grew to become Pershore Choral Society.

Mr Brown who owned the hardware store opposite Broad Street had three sons – the eldest of whom, Ronald, was a captain in the Army, Sid, and Graham who continued with the shop until relatively recently. This picture shows Sid Brown at a 1960s carnival.

It has been suggested the building occupied by the Working Men's Club was built on a site occupied by the Temperance Hall. Erected in 1847, this was the first National School. It was originally fronted by iron railings which were removed for use in the war effort during the Second World War. The club itself originated in Newlands, later moving to its present building. In 1921 the words '& Old Comrades' were added to its title. It has always had a history of letting rooms to other organisations and has thus played a useful role in the community for many years.

The Women's Land Army was founded prior to the Second World War with the idea that should war come, a women's organisation for helping with food production would be ready, and Lady Denman was appointed as Director by the Ministry of Agriculture. After training at an agricultural college or farm institute girls were sent to work at various farms at a wage of 28 /- for a 48-hour week. Avonbank – now the Horticultural College – became a hostel with others at Hurstmead and Summerfield at Birlingham. The organisation ceased in 1947. The picture shows the girls at Avonbank with Mr Young.

A wartime parade, possibly during Warship Week, with a saluting base by Burtons corner shop where High Street joins Broad Street. A sign set up over the door was divided into £10,000 sections with a target of £125,000.

During Warship Week (15-22 November 1941) an appeal was undertaken by Pershore Rural District Council and townsfolk to adopt the destroyer HMS *Scimitar*. Within five days £100,000 had been collected with a final total of £200,000. The week opened with a Grand Parade on 15 November, twenty-four organisations marching past a saluting dais erected in Broad Street. Dances were held at the Three Tuns and the Angel and a showing of 'Target for Tonight' with a variety concert took place at the Plaza (see page 24) for three nights. In addition the fire brigade and ambulance service gave demonstrations and stalls sold produce in Broad Street.

To commemorate the adoption, a plaque bearing the ship's arms was presented to the town while a smaller plaque bearing the town's arms was handed to the ship on 5 May 1943. In 1992 Pershore Town Council acquired the ship's bell as a gift from the Ministry of Defence in recognition of the long association between the ship and the town. Three years later a reunion between various members of the crew, including the captain, Robert D. Franks and some of the personnel rescued by the *Scimitar*, took place at Pershore Heritage Centre.

Nurses at Heathlands during the Second World War.

Ploughing at Revells, Woodfield Farm, Birlingham. A group of German POWs were billeted here and the photograph shows Heinz Wichmann working the field. Heinz later married a local girl and still resides in Pershore.

In 1941 a squadron of the Air Training Corps (ATC) was formed in Pershore. This picture shows the group taken outside the Senior School in Station Road two years later.

Pershore Cricket Club dinner, Angel Hotel, 1954. Among those pictured are Ken Emms, Ian Maple, Dave Barber, John Long, Derek Garside, Alf Hughes, ? Bomford, Graham and Sid Brown.

1st Pershore Brownie Pack, 1940s.

1st Pershore Company of Girl Guides, 1933, which consisted of Red Rose, Daffodil, Lily of the Valley and Violet patrols. From left to right: Nora Barber, Joan Davies, Mary Haines, Mary Howes, Peggy Champken, Doris Cowley, Betty Workman, Diana Newell, Margaret Champken, Edith Twigg, Mary Edgington, Joyce Hewlett, Frances Houghton, Gladys Turvey, Freda Bickerstaff, Marguerite Dufty, Mary Hartland, Nellie Reid, Esme Champken, Winnie Teale, Beatrice Arnold, Nellie Lee, Margery Hewlett, Joyce Teale, Elsie Middleton, Betty Overd, Violet Porter with Miss Joan Elkington (Captain) and Miss Meg Gammon.

In 1968 an exhibition (Legion '68) was held in the schoolroom of Pershore Baptist Church as part of that year's festival. Organised by the Royal British Legion and RAFA, the picture shows the exhibition chairman, Lt. Col. Newcombe (retired) and the patron, General Sir Richard Gale, late of the Worcestershire Regiment and Commander of the Airbourne Forces who landed on D Day, talking to Mr A.H. Annis, Group Chairman British Legion (Worcs) and Mr Revers.

Parade approaching the west door of the Abbey during the Worcester Royal British Legion County Rally at Pershore, 1968. The Pershore branch of the Legion was founded in 1922 under the patronage of General Sir Francis J. Davies. During the Second World War members were much involved with building up the ARP, Special Constabulary, Observer Corps and Home Guard and organising gift parcels for servicemen and women. Various fund-raising events took place including an annual Poppy Ball held at the Angel's Masonic Hall or the Three Tuns ballroom, in order to assist needy ex-servicemen and their families.

The Council offices decorated for the Coronation of Queen Elizabeth II on 2 June 1953.

On 25 May 1957 Princess Margaret attended a Girl Guide rally at Hindlip, Worcester, calling at Pershore en route. The photograph shows her leaving Broad Street.

Young Wives party, January 1961. From left to right, back row: Mr and Mrs Keel, Mr and Mrs Peart, Mr and Mrs Colori, Mr and Mrs Peters. Front row: Mrs and Mrs Taylor, -?-, Mr and Mrs Webster, Mr and Mrs Emerson. There being no Mothers Union, a Pershore Young Wives group was formed as an alternative in the 1950s. It met monthly at St Agatha's Hall. In the 1960s they moved to Abbey Park School and changed their name to Abbey Women's Fellowship. A further move took the group to St Andrew's Parish Centre.

A scene from *The Wanderer*, a play by R.H. Ward, especially commissioned for the Pershore Festival in 1962, showing Edwin Bick as a youth, Alec Johnston as the offender with Judith Thomas and Jacqueline Tricker as their girlfriends.

In 1874 the 9th Earl of Coventry re-founded the once-flourishing hunt at Croome using what had been a sort of menagerie at Croome Court to house the hounds. It has existed in its present form since 1899 when Hon H.T. Coventry and G.D. Smith purchased hounds from a Mr Rangham. In 1910 there were 50 couples of hounds, the Master being Lord Charles Bentinck. The meet at Pershore originally took place at the Star the morning following the Hunt Ball, later changing to Boxing Day. Broad Street was first used at as a meet in the 1960s.

The fire station (now Belle House and the Town Council office). The house behind the lamp post is No 5 Bridge Street, since 1955 the home of Pershore Heritage and History Society.

The arrival of the new fire engine at Mill Meadow, *c.* 1900. A Merryweather steam engine with a 150-ft high jet able to top the Abbey, with a quarter-mile of hose and dispensing 300 gallons per minute, it was the only one in the area able to control floods at Pitchcroft in 1924. It is thought the personnel are from left to right: Peter Hudson; ? MacCowan (Engineer); C.H. Field (Lieutenant); Mr Smith (2nd Lieutenant). Back row: Messrs G. Daniels, D. Twigg, B. Wright and R. Hook. The original engine was procured in 1900 with the help of public subscriptions from neighbouring villages – no subscriptions, no turnout! It was controlled by joint lighting and watching inspectors.

The fire engine leaving the station and passing the Three Tuns along Broad Street, *c.* 1900. It is said that on this occasion it was 'rushing' to Eckington where the thatch of a cottage had been set alight by a spark from a steam train. Having stopped for a photograph shot on the way, it is hardly surprising they arrived too late to save the cottage! Later Mr Partridge lent one of the mill lorries to pull the engine since the horses took some time to be rounded up and harnessed to the engine.

Five
Work and School

Pershore Fruit Market, Broad Street (facing High Street). In 1909, 400 growers combined to launch Pershore Co-operative Fruit Market. Although produce had been sold in Broad Street, previously, the procedure had been a rather haphazard affair. With the advent of the Co-op Fruit Market, the auction became more efficient with the first sale being held on 17 June 1909 and thereafter regularly until April 1910 when the first auction sheds opened in Defford Road.

Pershore Fruit Market, Broad Street (facing Defford Road). Pershore produce was famous throughout the country, being packed in baskets manufactured locally, in the main by Mr M.J. Spiers and his men in the grounds of 31 Bridge Street. Brought to the bottom of the garden in flat bottom punts, the bundles of osiers were boiled and pickled, then pressed, turned and skinned until only the white cane remained. These were then woven into pot hampers, chip baskets and soft fruit punnets, the men sitting on the floor in a circle as they worked, each pot hamper taking three to four hours to complete. Mr Spiers was a well-known Pershore person, being a Baptist lay preacher and running a gospel room in Newlands.

Sale of sheep and cattle in Broad Street, c. 1900. During the 18th century the date of the horse and cattle fair was changed to 26 June with a sheep and pleasure fair held in October. These took place in Holy Cross churchyard until 1836 when the sheep fair moved to Broad Street and the horse and cattle fair to Newlands. Later a livestock market was opened in Head Street.

The opening of the new auction sheds for the Co-op Market. In April 1910 the first auction sheds were officially opened by Mr Hooper. Built on the site of the old school house, there was a floor space of 16,000 sq. ft which was barely enough to house the amount of produce for sale. At times the line of horses and carts stretched as far as the bridges and to offload one's stock could take hours. The Carriers would therefore leave their horses to shuffle forward on their own, having first made certain their piles of baskets were topped by empties or were too high for a following horse to take a quick munch! Many disputes were caused by this practice!

The four 'Ps' painted on the sides of the baskets stood for 'Pershore Produce Properly Packed' and was the logo of the Co-operative Fruit Market. Cynical locals said it meant 'Pershore People Poorly Paid'.

The refreshment stall at Pershore Co-op fruit market. This postcard was signed by Lil and she notes that it was taken on 20 February 1919 stating that it was her 'hut and hobby', although most Pershore residents who recall this stall remember it belonging to Miss Gertie Hall.

Since much of the business carried on at the market was seasonal, in 1951 cold storage capacity of 6,500 bushels was introduced. In 1958 a subsidiary company, Abbey Produce Ltd, was set up for pre-packing fruit and vegetables using otherwise empty premises and redundant staff. On 17 June 1959 the Company celebrated its Golden Jubilee. At this time the General Manager was Mr W.E. Addison, the assistant manager was Mr J. Fagg and there was a staff of thirty-six.

Produce awaiting auction during the 1960s.

Produce being brought to the Co-operative market (later Pershore Growers Ltd), the entrance of which was to the left of the picture where the brick gatepost can be seen, 1940s.

Plum picking at the turn of the century. Following the discovery of the wild plum in Tiddesley Wood in 1833, trees were planted at Gig Bridge and by 1871 the Pershore (or Egg) plum was in production. In 1877 Walter Martin of Drakes Broughton transferred pollen from the purple 'Diamond' to the 'Rivers Early Prolific'. Five stones were planted – one of them growing. Martin's nephew, James Paynes of Lower Moor, took the first 25 grafts of 'Martin's Seedling', later known as the 'Pershore Purple'. Plum growing was undertaken with enthusiasm with a large selection of varieties and much of the land surrounding Pershore used as plum orchards. The last commercial plum grower in the town was Mr Westcott, Station Road.

Mrs Conly of The Grove was selling all manner of fruit when this order form was completed in August 1910.

Mrs. Conly thanks her numerous Customers for past favours, and has again much pleasure in submitting the following List of

Fruits and Prices.

The Fruits will be sent off FRESH PICKED, carefully selected and packed. Full nett weight of Fruit guaranteed in every Box. Carriage Paid, and Box Free.

Send P.O. with Order, please.—*Address :*

The ~~VIOLET~~ GROVE, PERSHORE, Worcester.

	6 lbs	12 lbs	24 lbs	36 lbs	
Plums (Pershore Egg)	2/-	3/3	5/3	8/-	Carriage Paid.
„ Victorias ...	2/3	4/-	7/-	10/6	
„ Greengages ..					
Damsons					
Blackberries					
	8 lbs	16 lbs	32 lbs	64 lbs	
Apples (Cooking)					
„ Baking					
„ Dessert					
Tomatoes ... .: ...					

A fine elm tree from Endon Hall Park near Pershore being moved to John Hickman & Sons, Wolverhampton. Nicholas Brothers, builders were in Bridge Street in 1910.

Hops were grown along Station Road and also at Wick. The canvas bins on a wooden framework were moved each day to the spot where picking would begin, strings were cut and laid across them for the papery, sulphur-smelling flowers to be plucked from the binds into the bins and measured by the bushel. Pickers were paid for the number of bushel baskets filled.

Abbey Garage, 1964. From 1871 until 1883 this was the site of Edward & Thomas Humphries' agricultural machinery works until it moved to Station Road. Taken over as a jam factory in the 1880s, the then manager, Arthur Beynon, began a series of auction sales in order to dispose of fruit surplus. When bankruptcy closed the Pomona Works the premises were brought for a garage business with the Central Market sharing the site. During the Second World War, when the Central Market purchased additional land, Bill Tarrant enlarged his garage. Petrol pumps now mark the site of the old market office and the shed where eggs were graded became the garage paint shop.

In 1840 Edward and Thomas Humphries set up an agricultural machinery works in High Street, moving to the site now occupied by the Abbey Garage in 1871. Their threshing and steam engines became famous and in 1885 this Atlas Works moved to the site of an old brickyard near Pershore station. This was subsequently owned by Messrs Bomford & Evershed, the Horsfall Destruction Company and Messrs Fisher Humphries before being acquired by Messrs W.H. Allen & Sons Ltd of Bedford in 1955.

A standard threshing machine working at Pensham farm during the Second World War with German prisoners working in the background. The gentleman in the hat is Mr Rowan, the farm manager with Bill Smith (arm outstretched). He is also pictured as a member of staff outside the International shop (see page 42).

W.H. Allen & Sons Engineering Works following their modernisation in 1965. The firm is now known as Allen Gears.

This view of the Victorian mill building, Bridge Street, clearly shows a top asbestos storey which was added during the Second World War when Britain had to maximise food production as part of the war effort. A mill at the south end of Bridge Street is known to have existed for many centuries. It is mentioned in the Domesday Book (1086) when its value was estimated at 4/-. From early times the building was under the jurisdiction of the Abbey but during the 15th century it was out of action with the monks having to grind their corn at Wyre Piddle Mill.

Back of the mill early this century. The advent of the canal age between 1700 and 1800 made the river navigable and enabled vast amounts of grain to be brought to the mill for grinding. A weir gate below the mill could be closed to raise the water for passing boats. However, this reduced power for the three water-wheels then probably in use, so a fee was levied. At the end of the 1800s millstones were largely superseded and horizontal rolls were installed.

One of the mill's early lorries. The mill continued to belong to the Ecclesiastical Commissioners until the 1930s. G. Partridge & Sons then took over when two turbines and a Robey diesel engine were installed but during its latter years the mill needed to diversify by dealing in animal food stuffs in addition to flour. By then bread was being baked by large factories and the days of the small millers were numbered.

The business continued to flourish until on 15 July 1976 the mill suffered a disastrous fire. Such fires were a constant cause for concern to mill owners since the dust created during the manufacture of flour and its by-products is extremely inflammable.

Gunston Hall Plantation, the home of George Mason (1725-1792) at Lorton, Virginia, USA. George Mason's great-great-grandfather was Thomas Mason who married Ann French in Pershore Abbey in February 1624. Their sons George and William fled to America after fighting on the Royalist side in the Civil War, landing there in 1651. The family prospered and George Mason became involved in Virginian politics writing the state's declaration of rights in 1776, a document which became the model for Jefferson's later Declaration of Independence.

The pulp and cider factory at the corner of New Road. This later became the firm 'Farm and Road' selling farm equipment and road-making materials before being taken over by the Delma Canning factory which employed displaced persons encamped around Broadway and Moreton in Marsh who were apt to be very volatile! Rossers, a firm making chocolate Easter eggs, used the premises before it became the factory shop.

102

The Epicure factory was situated on the site of the old White Horse brewery, 1960s. Founded by Col. Sykes, the factory produced fine hams with a special curing process using an old family recipe. Later, they expanded to sell faggots, sausage rolls and pasties, supplying the early motorway service stations.

The staff of the Epicure factory, July 1967. From left to right, back row: Sheila Howes, Bett Curly, Rose Ridge, Gwen Whittaker, Doug Hartland (manager), Glad Dixon, Lynn Young, Carol Bartlett. Front row: Stella Bartlett, Rosemary Message, Kath Townend, Grace Blow, Joan Jones. Cyril Curly took the photograph.

Preston House viewed on a small engraving made between 1829 and 1831 when a Mr Bushell bought the school here. In 1840 the school was considerably enlarged. It was one of several private academies which existed in the 19th century for both boys and girls, some of which took boarders.

The National School in Defford Road was surrounded by the Co-op Market. The boys' and girls' sections were separated by a house, and in the playground behind, by a wall. The County Senior School in Station Road (now the High School) eventually replaced the National School but the buildings were used as a Junior Mixed School until 1932 when another was built next to the infants' school in New Road. Built in 1840 for 400 children, in 1910 the Master was Mr W.T. Chapman with the Misses M. and G. Brickell as Mistresses of the Girls and Mixed Group. Each day began with prayers followed by a scripture lesson and the Vicar paid a weekly visit.

Class 1 at New Road Infants' School, 1928-29. Known as the Pershore County Council School (Infants), it was built in 1906. Until then the Infants had had to attend at three different centres: the Mission Hall, the Working Men's Club or the gymnasium. In 1910 Mrs E. Hutton was the Mistress here. Following the erection of a modern school to the rear, the building was used for some years as a kitchen for school meals but it was demolished in 1995 and a group of houses built in its place and named Betjamin Court, commemorating the interest paid to the town by Sir John Betjamin, the late Poet Laureate.

Church of England Junior School, 1931 with Class 2 girls and Class 1 boys.

In 1938, following the splitting of the premises from Stanhope House, Miss Young founded the Ley School with six pupils aged four to eleven years of age. Prior to that she had been a governess. She retired from the school in 1971 as did her assistant for 23 years, Mrs Elizabeth Kettle.

Staff at Ley School. From left to right, back row: -?-, -?-, Maureen Meredith, Pauline Barrow, -?-. Front row: Barbara Wall, Miss Jackson, Miss Young, Jan Browning. Miss Jackson took over as headmistress on the retirement of Miss Young and still holds the post today.

Mr Peter Hanson (1846-1932) who lived at Bedford House in Bridge Street opposite the draper's shop which he also owned (now Seal's). He was a well-known Pershore character, known locally as 'The Mayor', although at that time there was no official appointment to this title.

It is thought that this picture was taken during the mock mayor-making ceremony performed for Peter Hanson by friends, both local and from Birmingham.

Amerie Court, the home farm estate of the Abbey and the largest in the Manor of Allesborough, which once covered a much larger area than at present. In the 1790s the house was let as a residence and during that time Joseph Haydn is known to have been entertained to dinner there, writing a song to his hostess, Mrs Hodges.

Polly Cartland, with Barbara (born 1901) and Ronald (born 1907) at Amerie Court. Mrs Champken, Esme Westcott's mother became nanny to Barbara (later to become the world-famous romantic author) and her brothers Ronald and Tony who were both killed during the Second World War. A memorial to both sons, their father Major Bertie Cartland, who died in the First World War, and their mother Polly, who died in 1976 aged 98, stands near the gates of Tewkesbury Abbey. Barbara attended Mr and Mrs Brickell's School in Bridge Street and later Alice Ottley School in Worcester. Her daughter Raine later married Earl Spencer, father of Diana, Princess of Wales.

Polly Cartland continued to remember her children's nanny sending her cards each Christmas usually accompanied by a letter.

This picture taken in 1942 shows Barbara with her husband Hugh McCorquodale and their three children: Raine, Ian and Glen (in his mother's arms).

The funeral procession of the late Major Christopher Marriott of Avonbank, died 15 July 1908, passing along the main street at Wick. This was once the main London road, passing Wick House and running parallel to today's A44.

Six
Around the Villages

The villages around Pershore are as varied as their names suggest but all have their special charm and unique surroundings. History has certainly been writ large in the area, from the days of the Saxons, the Romans and the Civil War to the elegance of Georgian life and later. In the days of the Pershore Rural District Council there were 44 parishes within its scope – each in its own way worth a visit. Although a detailed explanation of them all is beyond the scope of this book, I have included a few pictures to whet your appetite.

Coventry Terrace, Pinvin, which was built by the 9th Earl of Coventry at about the same time as the Coventry Arms, presumably for workers at his nearby jam factory. In order that enough steam could be produced, water was drawn by hand from the stream alongside at 7am and 12 noon, the worker being given half a pint of rum and milk by the landlord of the Coventry Arms in payment.

Coach and Horses, Pinvin, thought to be a 16th-century coaching inn. In the orchard next-door (where bungalows now stand) plums were grown. Early this century Mr Edgar Morris was the landlord. Mr George Cox (born 1913 and the first name to appear in the 'new' register of christenings at Pinvin church) used to take donkey foals to the inn to be christened – everyone being obliged to drink to its health! During the Second World War the inn was extremely popular with airmen stationed at the nearby airfield. The main road which used to pass in front of the inn was diverted to its present position some years ago.

Roslyn Stores as it was early in the century when owned by Mrs Harris. A yew tree in the garden was regularly trimmed and the oil extracted from the timber was used to treat horses. Next-door there was a blacksmith's shop, the site of the present-day bungalow.

Boulter's Cottages, built 1853. Originally three cottages – the two shown and one built at the rear – tenanted by the Hall and Winters families and Albert Cook, they became one house in the 1960s. The three cottages in the background are Days Cottages which are even older.

The refreshment tent, Pinvin Sports. Many of the events staged in the village took place behind the Coventry Arms. Could the presence of the Union Jack point to this annual event being photographed in 1911 – the year of the Coronation of King George V.

Wyre Mill, *c*. 1904. There are records of a mill on this site for over a thousand years. On 18 May 1811 the foundation stone of a new building was laid by Mr T. Lloyd. This mill ceased trading in 1948 when C.D. Barwell OBE purchased the freehold. The building then became a social club and the headquarters for efforts to restore the navigability of the lower Avon.

The 500-year-old Anchor inn, Wyre Piddle, which originally marked the boundary of Wyre and Pershore, *c*. 1906. An old poem reads: 'There's Upton Snodsbury, Peopleton and Crowle; North Piddle, Wyre Piddle and Piddle in the Hole!' Most folk today tend to leave out the 'piddle' part of the name which refers to the brook which joins the Avon at this point.

There were two mills at Fladbury. This one, standing on an island between lock and weir was reached by a flat-bottomed boat pulled across the river by strong cable. Both mills were famous for their cider in addition to grinding flour. In 1899 Fladbury Electric Light and Power Co. was formed making the village one of the first to have electric lighting and power supplied to private houses.

The National School at Fladbury, *c.* 1905. This was erected in the Early Decorated style of architecture with houses alongside for the master and mistress. A more recent extension now adjoins the building.

Charlton, a short way from Cropthorne is an attractive village with the Merry Brook meandering parallel to the main road. This photograph dates from the 1960s.

Cropthorne has an abundance of black-and-white cottages and was mentioned in the Domesday Book. The church dates from Norman times and houses the head of a Saxon cross which was discovered forming part of the south wall in the 18th century. Originally 'Pound House', the 'old cottages' shown here acted as a post office c. 1906. During the First World War it was the only house in the village to possess a telephone.

Bredon Hill is an outlier of the main Cotswold range. On three sides there are extensive views – a position which was well suited to prehistoric occupation as seen in the remains of Kemerton Camp. Forest clearing took place on the lower slopes in the 14th and 15th centuries but it was not until the 20th century that land above 600 ft was cultivated. Stone from the hill was used to repair Worcester Cathedral after the Civil War and the hill was often used in past times for sporting functions.

The Royal Oak inn, Bredon, c. 1905. The butcher's shop next-door was incorporated into the inn building in the 1980s. In the 1950s the landlord was Bill Davis, who stayed thirteen years, followed by Ivor Brown for a further thirteen. To the right of the picture the horse-mounting steps (still there – just) can be seen. The building to the left was the old police station.

It is thought the site of the village cross at the entrance to Elmley Castle probably marks the focal point of the old market and square. Although dated 1148, it is thought to be some one hundred years younger. The cross, like all market crosses, would be the spot where circulating preachers would speak, where the proclamation of local and national news would take place and where agreements and bargains were made.

Elmley Castle is reputed to be one of the ten most beautiful villages in England. The earliest reference to it dates from 780 when King Offa granted land there to the church at Worcester although it seems it was settled some 160 years earlier. With the Norman invasion in 1066 Elmley passed to Robert d'Abitot, High Sheriff of the County. In the mid-12th century the castle at Elmley was extended and elaborated and became the chief seat of the Beauchamp family. Around this time a church was built, later extended, and a deer park enclosed to house a gift of animals from the king. The latter part of the 13th century saw the demise of the castle and thereafter it became a 'quarry' for local building.

The same main street taken from the Hill end of Elmley Castle village, 1960s. It is thought the main road owes its great width to the fairs and markets held there. Each Wednesday saw a market and there was an annual fair for two days on the Feast of St Lawrence and the day following (10-11 August). In 1575 the village received a visit from Elizabeth I. It is supposed she made a point of visiting her most affluent subjects because the cost of entertaining her and her retinue ensured none of them could grow too rich and powerful! The Queen Elizabeth public house shown in the picture commemorates this event.

The 'Big House' at the time of General Sir Francis Davies, born in 1864. The house was originally built in 1544 by the Savage family and it was where Elizabeth I was entertained. The Savage family remained here until 1821. In 1822 it was bought by T.H.H. Davies with various members of that family living there, until it was demolished in 1963. It is believed a small stone church, consisting of a chancel and nave, was built at the same time as the castle in 1086. This was extended in the 13th century and now contains not only Norman but Early English, Perpendicular and Decorated architecture.

THE CROSS, LITTLE COMBERTON. C92.

Rectory Cottage pictured here *c.* 1905 to the right is little changed today although houses have been built in the adjacent orchard. The signpost has been moved to the left, on the corner of Manor Lane, while a pleasant memorial garden has been formed on the corner where it originally stood.

LITTLE COMBERTON

Cottages in Manor Lane, restored and made more comfortable but showing little external change. Little Comberton life in the past revolved around the church and manor, the latter providing most of the water available. The well was kept padlocked and only opened for a short time each morning. It was General Sir F. Davies of Elmley who eventually piped spring water from Bredon Hill to the village.

A split-view postcard showing Eckington bridge, church, cross, cottages and weir. The origins of Eckington go back to Roman times but the oldest structure in the village is said to be the cross, used for preaching by monks from Pershore Abbey. The base and greater part of the shaft is all that remains of the original – the top was added during Victorian times.

The church dedicated to the Holy Trinity is late 12th-century with later additions, the tower being added in the 14th century. Inside is a large memorial to John Hanford, builder of Woollas Hall on the side of Bredon Hill, who died in 1616. This hall replaced one originally built in 1219 when a family called Musgros lived there. The Hanford family were staunch Catholics and a priest hole entered through a fireplace was constructed to hide the forbidden priests at the hall. Opposite the church is the old post office and shop cared for by M.A. Firkins.

The mill at Nafford, pictured here *c*. 1905, was an extensive building which originally formed part of the Manor of Nafford. It was granted by John de Birlingham to Alexander de Besford and Joan his wife in 1441-42.

Fire still smoulders in this picture of the ruins following a fire at Nafford mill on 17 May 1909. A nearby area is thought to have been the site of a church dedicated to St Katherine to which Birlingham church was a chapel. There was a priest at Nafford as early as 1086 but the building was in ruins by the 13th century and the true site is unknown today.

Croome Hunt meet at Nafford, 1910.

The river at this point has created a large bend and a weir has been created to siphon off some of the flow. Adjacent to the old mill site is a lock controlling the rise and fall of the river waters.

THE CHURCH AND OLD STOCKS, BIRLINGHAM.

This card, posted on 14 September 1910, shows the church and stocks at Birlingham. The churchyard looks to be very overgrown and a far cry from today's snowdrop and crocus-strewn swathes. The church of St James became the parish church after that at Nafford fell down. It was rebuilt in the Perpendicular style in 1870 when the Norman chancel arch was re-erected at the entrance to the churchyard.

The war memorial was erected in the churchyard following the First World War.

The lodge and school, Defford, *c.* 1905. This Victorian school was built in 1872 by Frederick Smith of Eckington with workmen walking from Pershore to the brick kilns in Croome Road, a quarter mile from the school, where the bricks were fired. The total cost of building was £861. 12s of which £500 was raised by subscriptions, the remainder through grants. School payments were: for the children of labourers (2*d* per week), children of parents between labourers and farmers (3*d*), children of farmers (6*d*), children of others (9*d*).

The lychgate and Institute, Defford, *c.* 1900. The Institute building has now been replaced by a brick building on the same site.

Defford church *c*. 1905. The church of St James was originally a chapelry of Pershore containing a chancel, nave, timber-framed 14th-century tower and three bells. Some of the windows date from the 16th century. It seems that occasionally 'quaint' characters were taken by photographers to various locations as this old man appears on several other postcards also!

The administrator's cottage, Besford Court, *c*. 1905. This house was granted by William the Conqueror to Urso d'Abitot. On his death it passed to his daughter Emaline until, with her marriage to Walter de Beauchamp, it became the property of the Besford family. In 1492 the Besford family line ended and the Court was taken over by the Harwells, the last of whom, Sir Edmund, was High Sheriff of Worcester. On his bankruptcy, Besford was sold to the Sebright family who owned in until 1885. George Noble, the owner from 1910, knocked down the Georgian part of the Court and built a mansion around an open quadrangle as an addition to the old house. Later, the building was converted into a school caring for and educating disadvantaged children under the auspices of the Catholic Church and carried out sterling work until 1996. The buildings are now in the hands of developers.

The drawing room, Wick (earlier Wyke) House. This, now demolished, house was at one time the home of Ltd Latimer and his wife Catherine Parr. It remained in its original state until 1730 when the front of the house became the back and two wings were extended westwards with stabling, servants' quarters and out-buildings. In the grounds was a large circular dovecote containing 1,320 nesting boxes.

Orchard Cottage is basically of a box-frame construction common in the 17th century, with indications of earlier, late-medieval origin. In its early days it was the homestead of a 70-acre copyhold farm stretching across today's A44 towards Little Comberton. It was home to the Archer family in the 1600s and to several generations of Smiths from the 1700s. More recently the cottage was divided into two separate houses. For many years the eastern end housed the village stores which closed c. 1960.

St Mary's, Wick, *c.* 1900. This was built in 1887 by Sir Aston Webb, who was also responsible for the Victoria Law Courts, Birmingham and the Victoria & Albert Museum in London amongst many other famous buildings. Webb was the nephew of Mrs Hilditch Evans, the wife of a former Wick churchwarden. It was at this house that Lord Haw Haw lodged during the 1930s.

The Forge or Smithy, Wick, 1890s. Successive generations of the Sherwood family were the blacksmiths here, with several of them serving as parish clerks.